SACRED AWAKENING INTEGRATION

Integrating Profound Psychedelic Experiences

Ian A. MacKenna

Sacred Awakening Integration

SAI

Copyright © 2022 Ian A. MacKenna

All rights reserved

Cover Art by: Grace MacKenna
gemvisuals.com

PREFACE

In this book we'll discuss some of the implications of the psychedelic therapy renaissance as well as techniques that may help someone in the aftermath of a particularly powerful psychedelic experience.

What we are learning these days is that intentional integration is absolutely necessary after a psychedelic experience of any magnitude in order to benefit the most from it as well as avoid disruptions to relationships and responsibilities. This is even more true after a full-blown transcendental experience, such as a peak Bufo or Ayahuasca experience.

I hope this information is beneficial for some.

-Ian A. MacKenna

INTRODUCTION

With the legitimization of psychedelic therapy exploding into the mainstream to treat PTSD, depression, and even fear of death itself, many people are looking toward psychedelics for wisdom, healing, or just a different perspective.

Ayahuasca, Psilocybin, and many other intriguing plant medicines as well as synthetic compounds have become part of the public discourse more than ever before.

I'm not here to advocate for psychedelics. Some however are called for whatever personal reason. What I can tell you is that profound subjectively spiritual experiences like these can be very powerful and also disorienting. This book is specifically focused on integration of peak life-changing psychedelic experiences.

There is no doubt that psychedelic therapies offer immense healing potential – it's not about getting high for a lot of people. Michael Pollan's book, *How to Change your Mind,* really brought it home that the desynchronizing effect of tryptamines, for example, like mushrooms and DMT, on brainwaves may be correlated with what is essentially a chance to shake off old neural patterns. From this new, kind of less-confined perspective, one may consciously forge new ways of thinking and behaviors. John C. Lilly called this metaprogramming.

Dissociatives like ketamine, for example, remove you from your body consciousness. With high doses that can literally be to the point of "Where did I leave my body?" And yet *you* still exist. So much trauma is held in our bodies. Imagine being free of that for a little while!

When you have the experience of being pure consciousness there is an opportunity to see who you really are and a profound bio-psycho-spiritual healing may occur, a kind of integration or defragmentation in and of itself. MDMA for PTSD, Ibogaine therapy for opiate addictions – there is some incredible research happening.

What's great about science is that it's dynamic, it's always evolving. When it comes to psychedelics specifically, a holistic approach is absolutely necessary to minimize dangers and maximize benefits, something that modern clinical research is confirming.

That means you don't just give someone with PTSD an ecstasy pill and hope it fixes their problem; That's just *not* how this all works. As it turns out, support before, during, and afterward is *absolutely necessary*. To have friends, perhaps family-members who care, and preferably at least someone who can actually understand what you're trying to express, such as a counselor familiar with psychedelic-assisted therapies.

Psychological models are about to evolve significantly. Think about all the traumas, neuroses, labels, memories, expectations, fears, doubts, shames and desires that people feel, how it weighs them down, how it stresses them out, which can manifest as many forms of dis-ease. And then imagine spending even a few minutes free of all that – just to remember for few minutes who and what you are – a conscious living *being*, awake, present, alive. That's what some of these medicines may offer. Maybe it's just that simple – being free of the body and everything it represents for a little while.

It should be no surprise that a psychoactive compound could have a lasting psychological effect, and there are hundreds of these compounds all with different effects.

The subjective experiences of the drug 5-MeO-DMT, for

example, are often described as "becoming one with universal consciousness" or the universe itself, or "remembering source", perhaps "seeing God", etc. Often people lose their fear of death entirely after such an experience; It can be the most profound 5-20 minutes of a person's life. And yet this is still largely uncharted territory!

The thing is... These experiences can be incredibly profound. They can be utterly terrifying or cathartic. Either way, often people have this time-transcendent conscious experience which completely reinforms their worldview, completely shifts their perspective on everything, who they are, what life is, what this *moment* is.

And then afterwards they – what – go back to their day job? Go back to the office? Go back to the morning commute as if nothing happened? It can be hard, but it's important to find a way to integrate. As a matter of fact that's what it's *all* about, bringing back these lessons and healing to your life so that you can embody them and be happier and more at peace, and then move on from there.

Not all of these medicines are so destabilizing by the way. MDMA for example doesn't tend to dissolve a person's whole identity as a human being like 5-MeO-DMT might. Although for some, that's exactly what we needed, to be free of even humanness for a few minutes, to know what it is to be pure consciousness. (5-MeO was very liberating for me but it's also undeniably pretty dangerous stuff.)

A common sort of response to what's considered a +4 experience on the Shulgin Scale is something like: "How can I live in this world after having an experience like this?" Feeling like you became one with God, etc. Tryptamines like DMT, 5-MeO-DMT, Ayahuasca, and other psychedelics like LSD are great at catalyzing these sort of +4 peak psychedelic experiences in certain contexts and for certain individuals.

> *PLUS FOUR, n. (++++) A rare and precious transcendental state, which has been called a "peak experience," a "religious experience," "divine transformation," a "state of Samadhi" and many other names in other cultures. It is not connected to the +1, +2, and +3 of the measuring of a drug's intensity. It is a state of bliss, a participation mystique, a connectedness with both the interior and exterior universes, which has come about after the ingestion of a psychedelic drug, but which is not necessarily repeatable with a subsequent ingestion of that same drug. If a drug (or technique or process) were ever to be discovered which would consistently produce a plus four experience in all human beings, it is conceivable that it would signal the ultimate evolution, and perhaps the end, of the human experiment.—Alexander Shulgin, PIHKAL*

Without proper preparation and integration support, however, the simple truth is that these peak experiences can be utterly devastating for a person's stability and mental health. One day you think you're Bob the Chef from Cincinnati, the next day you realize you're an eternal holographic fractal of consciousness that's one with the entire universe! How do you deal with that? With actually realizing that you're Neo? Buddha, whatever? (By the way, I am not here to say whether or not these subjective experiences are "true," that's really not the point – people *do* have these experiences. I've had a few myself.)

If you have a background in Taoism, Buddhism, Vedic perspectives, or even a general understanding of science, maybe the direct-realization of universal oneness might not be so shocking, but for some – maybe most – it usually is. They don't have words for it so they work with whatever psychological model can best cope with the experience of infinity.

If someone isn't ready it can be one of the most traumatic

experiences of their lives. (Obviously they shouldn't have taken the drug in the first place, or at least that dosage. Many other thresholds of carelessness had probably already been crossed by that point, possibly due to an unqualified facilitator.) But it does happen that people get way more than they bargained for, and it isn't pretty. Hopefully as society evolves people will become more educated and responsible in these matters and less people will be hurt in this way.

With proper support before, during, and after, these difficult trips can be integrated and unwanted disruption to a person's life can be minimized all *without* denying the realness and value of the *experience itself* as a life experience. It can be food for thought for a lifetime. And when a person actually IS ready, these experiences are potentially some of the most meaningful, profound, and beautiful of a lifetime.

Sometimes synchronicities, perceived meaningful coincidences, start popping up all over. Not everyone notices this, and for most that do, it isn't a problem – in fact it's great! – but for some people it can be very difficult when it feels like every dog barking in the distance is a reflection of your subconscious, every time a door closes just as you think a certain thought is a sign from the universe. It can be totally debilitating in some cases. If you haven't experienced that then you probably don't know what I'm talking about, but it happens to some. It's a beautiful and odd experience when it happens but can also be difficult to integrate when it feels like the external world really is reacting to your mind.

How do you deal with something that feels like a TRUE MYSTICAL AWAKENING, telepathic experiences etc – you might not necessarily *want* to shut it down... life *is* magical, why deny it? But you need to be able to cope right? To tie your shoes and function as a human being.

Integration specialists are critical in the emerging

psychedelic renaissance. And while more and more psychotherapists are beginning to recognize the potential value of psychedelics in therapy and adapting their models as needed, there are very rich shamanistic and mystical traditions which are increasingly relevant, having been used successfully for thousands of years to navigate these peak visionary experiences. (Like singing icaros, the sacred songs of an Ayahuascero to guide the trip, or the polyrhythmic drumming in Bwiti Iboga ceremonies which help synchronize the hemispheres of the brain.)

It's all about cultural integration these days as well, learning from the wisdom of the elders, the carriers of these medicines from ancient times to the present day. This is fragile knowledge, now in danger of being lost or diluted, even after having been maintained for thousands of years. And yet this wisdom has never been so accessible or necessary. The time to learn is now! Combine this folk-wisdom with modern medical knowledge and maybe you've got something.

> *"The schizophrenic is drowning in the same waters in which the mystic swims with delight."—Joseph Campbell*

As it turns out, these waters aren't uncharted after all. A great example is when the famous psychedelic hero of the 60s Timothy Leary wrote a translation of the Tibetan Book of the Dead, which is originally meant to describe the journey of the soul into the afterlife, translated into "psychedelicized English." He realized that the Tibetan Buddhist descriptions of the death-journey had close parallels to breakthrough psychedelic states, and that the wisdom of the Tibetan teachings was actually relevant and useful to navigate specific states of mind.

In fact, a morning meditation practice and some yoga

in the evening is probably some of the best preparation for the psychedelic journey. It isn't necessarily about what a person knows or doesn't know. Rather, successfully navigating psychedelic states may be much more dependent on internal energy systems, getting the body into a relaxed state, unifying mind and body through breath, and being able to do all of that intentionally. Conscious breathing can help you through some of the most spectacular moments of psychedelic experiences.

I'd like to discuss a few practical techniques that may help you or someone you know who has just had a profound spiritual experience and wants to work on integrating it into their daily life. I learned some of this information the hard way. These tips may help you spare yourself unnecessary suffering as you unfold into these new levels of awareness.

The important thing to keep in mind is this – it isn't really about the psychedelic experience itself – it's all about what you do with it. This is what Ayahuasceros call "the work." This is where you implement and embody your revelations, begin to stretch and grow into new levels of awareness in your daily life – and it *isn't necessarily easy.*

These simple techniques may help.

TECHNIQUE #1: VALIDATION

First – and this applies whether integrating your own spiritual experience or supporting someone you know – validation is important. So let's say someone has a *really* profound experience that transcends time and space, they see a vast white light that seems to be the universe or "God" and then they dissolve into that light for what feels like an eternity of bliss.

If someone tries to describe that experience to the average person, they will have no idea how to respond, and will either be amazed or call it crazy or delusional. It's important to above all recognize that what happened was just an experience of consciousness. We don't need to dismiss it as a meaningless hallucination, nor should we accept our interpretation of that experience as fact! These ecstatic states of mind are an amazing and mysterious facet of the human experience, whatever they "really" are!

So, first of all, your experience is an experience, your thoughts and feelings are valid as thoughts and feelings. Many people throughout history, and also many alive today, including myself, have felt similar things. I'm not even going to try to explain it away as a delusion. For me it's enough to just acknowledge the beauty of the mystery.

The first step to integration is to accept yourself, to

accept your experience, and recognize that all it is *is* experience, consciousness, your perception of your life; That's all you really have, that and your actions. It's okay to not understand everything right now. It is a beautiful, although sometimes disorienting, process. For what it's worth: Trust the process, even if it's uncomfortable; It's worth it.

It is absolutely critical to have proper support through every aspect of a psychedelic experience, before, during and after. Many counselors and psychologists are not yet familiar with psychedelic-assisted therapies and therefore may not be fully qualified to assist. In this case it may be helpful to reach out to a psychedelic integration coach in conjunction with whatever therapeutic modalities you are working with.

The emerging field of Psychedelic Integration fulfills the role of the shaman in contemporary psychedelic-assisted therapy, informed by ancient tradition as well as contemporary knowledge of psychology and pharmacology.

As it turns out, integration is what it's all about. A peak experience is surprisingly easy to "lose track of" if you don't take the time to process what happened, what it means, how to embody your new levels of awareness in your life. To get the most benefit from a psychedelic experience requires intention, otherwise it just becomes a memory of a bright white light.

And on the other hand, sometimes the experience is *too much*. It should never happen, but it does, sometimes due to an irresponsible facilitator, that people are overwhelmed. A "bad trip" can be the single most traumatic experience of a person's life. In these situations, working with a qualified psychedelic integration coach – preferably someone who has gone through it themselves and managed to fully integrate the experience – is absolutely critical. (Experienced trippers may scoff at this idea, but keep in mind that we're specifically talking about psychedelic-assisted therapy. Many people these days are new to psychedelics.)

It's long been said in psychedelic communities that, "There are no bad trips." What that means is: Upon successful integration of even the most difficult experiences, there is wisdom and healing to be attained. A common hallucination in high-dose Ayahuasca trips, for example, is seeing your own body dismembered, the pieces scattered in space. Obviously this imagery is disturbing if one isn't prepared for it, but to call it a "bad trip" is a vast oversimplification. As one dives into the shadow work of their own psychology, they may begin to see that their life actually *is* scattered and dismembered, and that this message is critically important to receive so they can begin to "get their life back together." Upon successful integration, most people don't regret even their most uncomfortable experiences. How could they? They are often some of the most valuable lessons of a lifetime.

So step one is validation, to accept that you had an *experience*. As strange or wonderful or even devastating as it might have been, there is no rush to interpret it! Now is a good time to pay attention to your feelings, to let your new levels of awareness unfold naturally.

Blessings!

TECHNIQUE #2: MEDITATION

What often happens is that someone has an experience bigger than words, bigger than the mind itself. Pure consciousness doesn't require "thoughts" to exist. And then afterwards the mind, the thoughts, the very thing that *separates you* from this simple *beingness* comes back into the picture and starts labeling it, "SO WHAT HAPPENED IS MY EGO JUST COLLAPSED INTO FRACTALS AND I BECAME ONE WITH THE UNIVERSE AND TIME DIDN'T EXIST AND-"... trying to compartmentalize *infinity* – it's a joke!

Zen Buddhism-style meditation teaches us to observe our thoughts and not identify with them. Having the thought "I am Bob" doesn't actually make you Bob. That is just a thought and "Bob" is just a label. What you really *are* is beyond all those descriptions, and after a serious trip people confuse the thoughts *afterward* with the "vibrational essence" of the trip itself.

Remember, even the thought, "I am one with the universe, I am source," is a thought. And thoughts are okay, they aren't *bad*, but they are just thoughts, labels. They are not the underlying Truth itself that the labels refer to. (This is not to discount the profound revelations that may occur during and after this time that may very well be worth writing down, so-to-speak.)

If you already have a daily meditation practice, great! If you don't, here's an easy way to start:

What I suggest is a very simple meditation style. It's called the lazy-man's style. They call it lazy, because it works and isn't difficult. I practice this style of meditation every day first thing in the morning. I wake up and I go for a short walk. I prefer nature but if nature isn't very accessible to you, whatever comfortable private space you can find is perfect.

Sit down in a comfortable position, either in lotus, the lazy-man's position, or sitting down on a recliner. Rest your hands on your legs and breathe slowly. Be aware of your breathing, be present. If you have any thoughts, don't resist them. This is key! Just observe them, and *gently* let them go.

In the beginning it can be helpful to set a timer on your phone for 10 minutes. That's it! Just ten minutes of sitting, existing, observing your thoughts without stirring them up or adding to them. Sometimes with this practice you may find that you "thought" the entire time, especially in the beginning – that's okay!! Go about your day. The next day, you can try it again. Just ten minutes of just existing! And it's okay if you think the whole time again! There's nothing to prove in meditation! You're just witnessing.

If your dog walks up to you, you don't have to ignore it cause you're *meditating* – go ahead and pet it, and gently tell it to go lay down. The point is to let vibrations settle naturally. If you're in nature meditating and a beautiful hummingbird appears in front of you, observe that magical moment! The point isn't to dissociate from reality and "achieve the void." None of this is useful unless it helps you to be present, to enhance your connection and effectiveness in this world! Appreciate the hummingbird! If your sister calls you on the phone, it's okay to answer.

The beauty of this style of meditation is that it *can't* be interrupted. If something interrupts you, it's just part of the moment. Feel the calm of the meditative state and carry that into the rest of your day. You're already in the flow, every moment is the flow.

This simple habit quickly becomes very powerful. It's sort of like doing push-ups. I'm physically active. I know I could do 50 push-ups right now. But if I wanted to get into a daily habit again I'd just set out to do 10 push-ups a day. That way you don't get burnt out on it! It's an achievable goal! Then one day, after a week, I'd just feel like doing more, and I'd do 20 or 30. And then if I wanted to, I'd up the goal from 10 to 20 push-ups a day... but no rush.

Same with meditation. It's great to start with an achievable goal, and to not take it too seriously. Don't beat yourself up if you miss a day, or a week even. It's just a goal, a light-hearted practice. Just ten minutes a day of existing. You may find yourself going pretty deep before long. This method is nice because you don't create the sense of anxiety rooted in an expectation that you have to sit in some complicated posture for hours or achieve some specific mental state. The point is to relax the body-mind. The benefits of this practice cannot be overstated. It quickly becomes very powerful and can help you to transform every aspect of your life.

Just give yourself permission to exist, let yourself breathe, let yourself be present, let your thoughts settle like murkiness in a pond.

I usually end my morning meditation with 3 Oms. Omming is a timeless visionary navigation technique as well. Omming is simple! It is associated with many religious traditions, but when it comes down to it, it's just vibration.

After a couple of deep breaths, allow the Om, to rise from your abdomen. The spelling "Aum" describes the three phases of the Om. The beginning may sound like an "Ah" or "Oh" sound. As the Om progresses, the sound transitions to an "Oh" or "Ooh" sound, and finally your lips gently meet to form the "Mm" sound as you finish the tone with the last of your breath.

Omming isn't about how deep you can Om, or how loud or anything like that. The way I Om these days is by listening to the universe, listening to the energy around me, and then Omming *with* that energy, letting my attention merge with my surroundings. It's an acoustic resonance phenomenon. Even if the universe sounds disharmonious, like traffic in the background, etc, you can Om in a frequency that harmonizes everything just by letting your attention settle on that possibility, by "listening for peace" while you Om. I Om 3 times, breathing gently in between each time. Then when I'm finished I enjoy the afterglow for a minute or so and that's the morning meditation routine.

This ONE daily meditation practice can change your life on so many levels, increase peace as well as the depth of your spirituality *without* losing touch with reality – in fact it functions to enhance your connection with reality, bringing yourself consciously – *acoustically even* – into harmony with the universe.

TECHNIQUE #3: DO THE WORK

Whatever insights or revelations you experienced in that non-ordinary state may continue to simmer up over the coming days or even years. Please give yourself permission to feel these things fully. Especially in the days or weeks after a really deep experience, it's important to have quiet space to reflect, and simple daily activities that keep your mind and body in harmony while you reorganize your perspective.

Some physical activities that are great for this integration period are being in nature, hiking, gardening, yoga, dance, qigong. Perhaps you'll realize that painting or learning to play music, or playing more music, or maybe learning about herbs would be a beautiful shift in your life. Now is the perfect time to implement these changes. These ancient elemental practices can nurture your soul during that tender period as you reassess your life's purpose and trajectory.

Simplifying your diet, eating more wholesome foods, drinking more water... the importance of these simple things cannot be understated during this time. (Seriously, did you drink a glass of water today?) Body-mind harmony is critical for well-being.

So in these simple ways you can begin to shift the vibration of your life toward harmony and presence. And you'll feel the momentum shifting. You don't feel how fast you're going in a car but you can feel acceleration and braking. If you begin to accelerate your life, you'll feel it, and it feels *good*.

You may be experiencing emotional shifts. Emotions are raw, not always easy, but they are beautiful and it's okay to feel them. Try to make sure you have a safe place to feel these waves fully. You'll make it through.

By now it should be clearer what aspects of your life require your attention. It could be a relationship dynamic that needs to be addressed, the need to quit drugs or alcohol, the need to watch less TV. The key here is to implement these shifts gently. Be easy on yourself, ask for the support of your family and friends, and then *gently* make the changes you need to make in your life!

You probably shouldn't make any dramatic life changes while you're under the influence of the psychedelic as well as for a period of time afterward. That's part of a having good safe container: To set aside a time that you can call sacred, including an integration period, in which you don't make any major life decisions. But *after* that period, maybe you decide you really do want to get in touch with your brother and heal some family wound, for example. Do it, even if it's hard, if it truly feels right to you. Meditate, feel the peace of the clouds, and be invincible in your vulnerability, and say what you need to say, and listen with no expectations, and *do the work* of healing your life. Forgiveness, for example, is for you, not the person you forgive, it's to free yourself from the burden, to take back your power.

Once you consciously take your "homework" on as a project that you are enthusiastically passionately involved with, everything begins to change. All that trauma that has followed you around for years – when you begin to truly consciously face it, it's like paying off a debt, balancing your karma – and suddenly you're free in your own mind to choose your path from a less clouded, burdened perspective.

The point is to *do the work*, whatever that means to you.

In a therapeutic setting, dosages of these substances are administered responsibly, but sometimes people seek these experiences on their own and take it way farther than is responsible, and their ego-identity gets smashed to bits. They start "receiving transmissions" and seeing signs and it can be a real mess, even if it's manically beautiful to the person experiencing it. If that is you – and I've been there – your work FIRST AND FOREMOST is grounding. Bring that cosmic light down, channel it into your body, and emanate it here on earth. That means being able to tie your shoes, take care of yourself. It's hard coming back to the mundane from a divine perspective, but as that divine perspective becomes more integrated into daily life it *encompasses* the mundane. Turns out the mundane was divine all along.

There are some good tricks if you accidentally ended up a bit more enlightened than you planned to. So, for example, let's say you feel compelled to help awaken the sleeping masses to the illusion of reality, the nature of Maya, or something. That's admirable! Of course someone experiencing bliss and universal consciousness would want to share that.

But the thing is that individuals have their own karma, even if on another level we're all one. Eventually you might think of people who seem "unawake" more like kids and decide that they need to enjoy their childhood, play the games of society and materialism for a while until they themselves feel the call. It's not your place to disrupt that. Shattering people's illusions before they are ready can be absolutely destructive. You don't need to help a butterfly from its cocoon.

And besides, words aren't usually the best medium for this sort of communication. For people that are experiencing something that feels like enlightenment, I suggest refining your psychic abilities. (Sounds crazy, but if you know, you know.) That way when you buy some vegetables at the store, you can simply resonate on a particular frequency and without saying *anything* you can share your vibrational *darshan*. (A "darshan" is a blessing received from seeing a saint, just seeing the way a true saint or yogi moves, even for a few seconds, which can refine a person's own vibrations in profound ways.) So resonate at your highest, calmest, most grounded and loving wavelength, and you don't need to tell anyone anything – they just feel it. Most communication is nonverbal anyway.

What eventually happens is that, all of these spectacular miracles and revelations become... ordinary! So it's okay to relax a bit. You figured it out! You're one with the universe! (hint: you always have been) It's okay, you're beautiful. And if it seems like you are the center of the universe... That's because you *are* the center of your own universe! The universe seems to align just for you because you *really are special.* Now can you use your heart to truly see that in other people? In every single moment? The world becomes 7.9 billion times more magical when you realize everyone else is just as infinitely magical as you.

I'll let you in on a metaphysical secret, this is straight up internal mental alchemy. *'Namaste' means something like I honor the place in you, that when you are in that place within yourself, and I am in that place within myself, there is only one of us.* I try to keep grounded in the Western perspective so that people can understand what is being said here in language that is familiar to them, but here's a little Eastern mysticism for you.

The heart chakra, the Anahata chakra, is said to resonate with the entire universe. Therefore the energy you project into another person's heart chakra will manifest in your entire universe. So project the highest frequency of love, with as little expectation and judgment as possible toward every person you meet; Love the way you want to be loved by the universe itself. Really think about it, and embody that. See everyone else as the Universe Embodied, and the circuit of enlightenment is activated, funnily enough, it turns out you're really loving yourself.

So the key is to be easy on yourself, and even not take the whole process too seriously. If you have just experienced a profound awakening, congratulations! Truly! Although... It's nothing to brag about. In fact, humility is required now more than ever. You *don't* necessarily have to be all dramatic about it. That's how a Westerner who isn't grounded in these simple truths behaves. Of *course* you're one with the universe, which is a fractal holographic ocean of consciousness. People have been shouting it for thousands of years. The yogis were right! If you're paying attention, as you continue on your path, you'll see it in other people's eyes too. Many of us *know.* It's not like it's a secret, it's just that most aren't willing to see the truth. Now what are you going to do with it?

TECHNIQUE #4: FIND THE OTHERS

I know what it's like to live in a city, to be surrounded by friends and family who could never possibly understand why a person would want to drink a hallucinogenic Amazonian brew, for example, that makes you puke your guts out and possibly experience terrifying visions for 6 or more hours – and for *healing*?

And yet the paradigm is shifting *rapidly*. Millions of people are talking about these things. There are tons of psychedelic integration support groups online these days, often specialized for a particular substance.

5-MeO-DMT experiences are particularly profound and have a tendency to cause so-called 'reactivations' in the weeks and months after the initial trip. This can be pleasant for some or very uncomfortable but there are lots of 5-MeO-DMT integration groups where people can meet online that are having similar experiences.

Knowing you're not alone – in fact, knowing that we're all a part of this incredible awakening *together* – can really dispel the hopelessness of being misunderstood. We've never been so connected. So let's connect, let's meet each other, let's do this!

With care of legality, write your stories, tell your tales, share your revelations, and if your experience generated more questions than answers, we want to know! I want to know! I love hearing about people's peak psychedelic experiences, the ones that really shift their perspectives on life the universe and everything.

Regarding Shamans:

Beware of shamans! The trendy "shamans" selling peak experiences for $300 bucks that think that they're qualified to be so careless with people's minds are dangerous. Many are completely unqualified with no medical training whatsoever and it's completely unethical, even if they think they're some kind of prophet or healer. Know this: Psychedelic experiences are no guarantee of spiritual progress. Something that brings peace and comfort to 20 people could trigger a complete schizophrenic break in someone else with undiagnosed underlying mental illness. It can actually ruin someone's life, so don't take it lightly. Don't be that guy, please.

Also, this is of course a touchy subject, so be very careful of legality and (obviously) don't try to buy or sell illegal substances online. And be VERY careful about who you trust. Many people do want to take advantage of others by claiming some spiritual credentials, going after your money or even taking advantage sexually while someone is under the influence. This is big in Ayahuasca tourism in South America right now, so be careful. Read articles. It's good to connect with people but, in my opinion, be very cautious about anyone who calls themselves a shaman. I do really appreciate the Shipibo Ayahuasca traditions, the true Ayauasceros, but it's all too easy for someone who wants your money to wear a Shipibo-print shirt, shake a rattle, and offer to "heal you" for $3000.

There are some incredible facilitators by the way, but discernment is key. We're finding our way, and although we have some traditions to lean on, people still make mistakes. People don't realize how powerful these things are until they've pushed it too far and that can hurt people. And yet, good, humble work *is* being done on the front lines that is saving people's lives by facilitators that have paid dearly for their skills, and made mistakes along the way.

Some of the pioneers weren't fully qualified, but were too compassionate not to get involved, to not to try to make the world a better place while they were told to wait for laws and therapeutic protocols to catch up; People need help *now.* A few of these pioneers really did have the discipline and humility to truly learn their craft, learn from their mistakes, and learn from each other and have actually become some of the most qualified people on the planet to work with people using these substances. They are our elders and they have wisdom to teach us.

Regarding Becoming a Shaman:
The only shaman I trust is a reluctant shaman. Someone who truly knows how serious of an endeavor doing a deep soul \psyche-dive can be, someone who truly knows the risks. If you've blasted off on DMT ten times and eaten ten-strips of acid plenty of times or even smoked a bowl of salvia, you are STILL NOT QUALIFIED to be a shaman, so just *don't do it*. Just because you saved someone's life with CPR doesn't make you a heart-surgeon. If you think you've seen it all, I'm telling you, you haven't. And ego about being a shaman is a sure sign that one has yet to be truly humbled, and thus truly initiated. If you're pushing these things on people you *don't get it*. If you've never had an absolutely hellish ride, and then twenty more of them, really gotten to know the meaning of the words "shadow work" you are *not qualified.* A true shaman needs to know what could potentially happen to someone's psyche under the influence of a mind-manifesting drug that they aren't ready for, how to avoid that situation completely or at least help them through it if it happens because they've been through experiences like that themself.

In general, it's probably best not to even encourage people

to take psychedelics. Encourage research, have an open dialogue, share your experiences, sure, but please don't be pushy about it. It's an individual's choice; Some are called. Psychedelics are *not* a panacea... They are very, *very* dangerous. There are drug contraindications that are important to know about, for example, and people aren't always forthcoming about being on psych meds, so taking it upon yourself to go "turn on" people is highly irresponsible; You could kill them. Do you know how monoamine oxidase inhibitors interact with serotonergic drugs?

There are people already doing psychedelic medicine work, really deep people that have been at it for decades, trying to heal the world, that have studied with the Bwiti or the Shipibo. There are elders to learn from. Even if you think you see a better way, there are subtle nuances and distilled lessons to learn from those that have walked this road far longer than us. TRUE humility is called for in these circumstances.

Go to school if you want to do that work. Study neuroscience, chemistry and psychology, and dedicate yourself to it with as much discipline as any PhD. If your call is truly to devote your life to healing, to working with a particular medicine, my advice is to patiently cultivate a relationship with that medicine and the people that know it best, with utmost humility. If you are sincere enough, you will find the teachers that you need to; They will find you; They need you too. The work is never done.

Communicating and connecting with people with common interests and experiences in integration and support groups is a great decision. You may make some beautiful lifelong connections with people as magical as you, but also remember that it's okay to take it slow and be cautious. It's still the internet, so beware of charlatans and scammers, and try to keep it legal.

So speak your truth, be prepared to listen and learn, and find your tribe!

TECHNIQUE #5: MOVING ON

Now that you've accessed this feeling of universal consciousness it's time to express it in your life. True satisfaction is the result of a meaningful life, a life well-lived. Let's get real. There's not enough money, weed, sex or drugs in the world to provide true contentment. The only true satisfaction in life is in living with purpose. Like it or not – and I'm not going to cite my sources here – the ONLY way to truly be satisfied in this lifetime (something that is far greater than transient moments of happiness) is to **live your life well**.

That means looking at your life with radical honesty. You've had a taste of transcendence now, or perhaps a taste of the fire. Either way, there's only one way forward and that is to live your life with total conviction. Be whatever it is you know the world needs. You are so powerful!

That can be whatever it means to you. Maybe the hero the world needs is for you to be the best Dad you can be, to get control of your anger and quit smoking cigarettes. Or maybe you realize that wasting your life playing video games is actually morally reprehensible when so many people are suffering and that you actually *could* do something to make the world a better place if you weren't so self-centered. (Sorry if I'm calling anyone out, it's a common revelation.)

I know an 83 year old woman that does more good

community work in one week than some people do in their lifetime – and she does that *every week.* She's so good it's intimidating. And you just can't bring yourself to make excuses for why you're not as dedicated as she is to making the world a better place. You just see how *good* she is and know that you have to do that too, to dedicate your whole being to what *needs to be done.*

There are BIG PROBLEMS in the world: Fentanyl, meth, gun violence, poverty, homelessness, mental health issues, environmental issues. There are even bigger problems on the horizon. We need all hands on deck. That's the reality of the situation. Artists, inventors, community servants, teachers, carpenters. Whatever your passion is, find your calling and dedicate every atom of your being to your goal. 99% won't be enough.

If this sounds intimidating... Of course it is. But I'll tell you right now that the rewards are beyond comprehension. The universe reaches out to you, empowers you; Other people who live their life this way will see that look in your eyes and support you in everything that you do. Incredible things will unfold all around you because you're awake enough to see them. You're a person living for others, living for the Whole, and so the Whole supports you.

The point is this: It was never about the trip. It was never about the psychedelic. It's about you. It's about the alchemy of the soul, refining yourself in every area that you can, always. Seeking to embody your own highest ideal of yourself, to master yourself.

Cultivating love, peace, joy, vitality, dedication, discipline, loyalty, strength, faith, courage, focus, awareness, sensitivity, intelligence, kindness, communication, creativity, community... with every bit of your being. Taking on this impossible challenge will nourish you, lift you up, and that will in turn - to use the hippie colloquialism - raise the vibe on earth.

And when your journey becomes true medicine for others...
That's how you know you've made it.

Thank you for reading.
Blessings to you on your journey.

-Ian A. MacKenna

ACKNOWLEDGEMENTS

I would like to thank first and foremost my Dad who provided me with the inspiration to always seek truth on my own, even in the face of multitudes of people who claim to possess it. I'd like to acknowledge some of my biggest heroes: Carl Jung, Terence McKenna, Ram Dass and many other foreward thinkers. And a big thank you to the community of NSJ; You were my most important education.

ABOUT THE AUTHOR

Ian A. MacKenna

Ian has been fascinated by psychedelics and altered states of consciousness since he was a child. This curiosity brought him to study all forms of spirituality and mysticism that he encountered. He has over 16 years of experience assisting people with integration of psychedelic experiences. He currently lives in Tucson, AZ with his two dogs where he works as a carpenter and runs a psychedelic integration coaching service, and is an advocate for ibogaine research to treat addiction. He has personally assisted well over 100 people in their process of psychedelic and spiritual integration.

THANK YOU

If you or someone you know could benefit from psychedelic integration sessions please reach out at:

UbuntuUluru@gmail.com

REQUEST FOR SUPPORT!

SAI is working with a small team of independent researchers to **END THE OPIOID EPIDEMIC** through working toward sustainable sourcing of ibogaine. This is some of the most important work being done on the planet. You can join us by donating directly through CashApp or to our Ethereum wallet.

Cashapp: $UbuntuUluru
ETH:

0xE7f05D7d9A00634050e301BAF93F3dA9b54C0a72

Thank you for your consideration!

Printed in Great Britain
by Amazon